Find Your Voice

A Guide to Self-Expression

by

Zetta Elliott

Rosetta
Press

"Find your own voice and use it.

Use your own voice and find it."

~ Jayne Cortez

Table of Contents

How I Found My Voice..1

A Thousand Words...3

The Real Me Wreath...4

Soak Your Sponge...5

Create a Cloud..6

Prose or Poetry?..11

Make a List...15

Savor Each Season...17

Free Verse...22

Star Power..29

Write a Letter...34

Extract the Essence..36

Honor an Ancestor...38

Honor Wreath..43

Take a Stand...44

Ten-Day Poetry Challenge..47

Doodle!..58

How I Found My Voice

It took a long time for me to claim my identity as a writer. I didn't think I had the right to call myself a writer until I'd been published, and that took a long time. I now have over thirty books and in 2018 I wrote *Say Her Name*, my first poetry collection. In the foreword I admitted that I didn't think of myself as a poet, but what else do you call someone who has written over fifty poems? Once again I wasn't sure I was good enough to call myself a poet. I didn't have the same experience or passion as my poet friends and because I was comparing myself to others, I didn't allow myself to claim that identity.

In a way, this book is for my younger self. I wish I'd had a simple guide like this when as a teen I struggled—and failed—to write my first novel. Back then I was trying to mimic my favorite authors, and I didn't write about my own life because it seemed dull and insignificant. When I graduated from college and finally started reading the work of Black women writers, I realized that *every* life is worth writing about and each writer has a unique voice.

I made a sign and hung it above my desk: "Don't write what's expedient, write what's true." I stopped trying to sound like someone else. I worried less about pleasing or impressing my reader. Instead I tried to be as precise as possible when I was writing about my feelings. Some of the things I wrote were inconvenient to others, but I meant every word. Over time I began to write with less hesitation; I didn't agonize over every word. I'd found my authentic voice!

This workbook is for anyone who wants to write and just needs a little encouragement to get started. If you dream about writing a novel or a book of poetry, you'll first need to build up your stamina. Just as you train for months in order to run a marathon, it takes time and discipline to develop a writing practice. Think of your imagination as a muscle that needs daily exercise!

For National Poetry Month I decided to join thousands of other people in writing a poem a day for the month of April. It wasn't easy, but I kept in mind a poet friend's excellent advice—"Celebrate every poem whether it's brilliant or not, don't worry if you miss a day, and know that you can always revise your poems once the challenge is over."

Some of the poems I wrote during that month are included in this guide. I'm going to polish the rougher poems and even though NaPoWriMo is over, I might try to keep going! I've included a seven-day poetry challenge at the back of this workbook and encourage you to give it a try. When you commit to writing a poem every day, you're giving yourself permission to be creative. You're also carving out space in your life for self-expression, making it a priority.

I never met a writer when I was a child, but I know that I embody possibility when I walk into a classroom. While conducting writing workshops in schools, I often see the shine in a child's eyes as they realize that they can do what I do. I wrote this short poem after visiting a middle school in Harlem:

see me
be me
know we
can be
anything

Everyone has a story to tell. You can use words, paint, film, clay, and countless other ways to express yourself. Just give yourself the chance to experiment, explore, and find your voice.

Write on!

Zetta

A Thousand Words

They say that's what a picture is worth, but sometimes a photograph can't capture all of who we are. For the cover of this book, I asked artist Sonja Oldenburg to make a wreath using my favorite colors, flowers, and creatures. She also included objects that represent my roots: a red maple leaf for Canada, a starfish and a cowrie shell to represent the Caribbean and Africa. As an immigrant I identify with migrating creatures like butterflies and hummingbirds; the fairies and dragons reflect my love of all things magical. The four words represent my life as a writer: creativity, imagination, reflection, and dreams.

Make a "real me wreath" on the opposite page that shows who you have been, who you are today, and who you'd like to become. You can draw pictures of yourself and the people or things you love; you can also cut photographs out of magazines to create a collage. Here's a list of things you can include:

1. Your favorite colors: _____

2. Your favorite creatures: _____

3. Your place(s) of origin: _____

4. Your best traits: _____

5. Your favorite activities: _____

6. Your roles & goals: _____

The Real Me Wreath

Soak Your Sponge

I like to think of my imagination as a sponge that I use to soak up ideas. When my sponge is fully soaked, I wring it out and write down the ideas I've collected. Sometimes writer's block just means I've let my sponge dry out. Here are some ways you can get ready to write:

1. Spend time in nature. Being near trees always makes me quiet and then I see and hear things I might otherwise have missed.

2. Absorb art. Stopping for a moment to appreciate a mural on a wall does as much for my imagination as spending two hours in a museum.

3. Study stories. Read, go see a play, check out a matinee. Sometimes I watch a movie or TV show twice so I can study how the plot unfolds the second time around.

4. Set the mood with a ritual. Light a candle, burn some incense, or put on your favorite t-shirt. I used to wear lipstick when I wrote! It was something out of the ordinary to signal that I was shifting from one mode of being to another.

5. Create a quiet corner in your home that's dedicated to writing. We can't all afford "a room of one's own," but a comfy chair by a window or a table with a vase of fresh flowers will do.

6. Tune in or tune out. Sometimes I write to music, sometimes I write with the TV on, and other times I choose silence. Background noise can force me to focus but it can also be a distraction.

7. Order in. I signed up for the poem-a-day service from the Academy of American Poets. I start each day by reading a poem delivered straight to my inbox—for free!

Create a Cloud

It's easier to write when you have words at your fingertips. One of my favorite warm-ups is word association. When I'm leading a writing workshop, I give my students one word and one minute to write down all the words that pop into their head. For example, this is what they think of when I say the word "school"—desk, student, pencil, stress, friends, boring, future, science, math, etc. When the time is up, I ask for volunteers to share their words and I write them all on the board. Collectively we create a word cloud, which then provides vocabulary for our writing activity.

You can make your own word cloud with or without a timer. Think about the words on the following pages and write down whatever pops into your mind. Try not to censor yourself—give your mind the freedom it needs to offer up honest responses. If you do this warm-up with a friend, you can share your words and make an even bigger cloud.

love

home

spring

red

Prose or Poetry?

What is a poem? When we're writing prose, we make paragraphs with complete sentences that start with a capital letter and end with punctuation. The rules that apply to prose don't generally apply to poetry. But if you simply broke a sentence into fragments, would that automatically make it a poem? What makes poetry *poetic*?

PROSE is written in complete sentences:

> My grandmother took me to Coney Island.
> We ate cotton candy on the boardwalk.

Those two sentences use plain language to tell a simple story in a direct way. To turn **PROSE** into **POETRY**, we can extract the *essence* of our sentences and use it to write a free verse poem that has more descriptive language:

> the summer sun
> burning in the sky
> salty sea breeze
> wooden boards creaking
> beneath our flip-flopped feet
> sea gulls squawking
> my hand held in yours
> your smile sweet as
> cotton candy

Alliteration is the repetition of an initial consonant sound.

> summer sun
> salty sea
> cotton candy
> flip flop

You can use alliteration to create a pleasing effect for the reader of your poem. I wrote a haiku that I liked, but then I revised it to add more alliteration (<u>ch</u>imes/<u>ch</u>urch, <u>b</u>ells/<u>b</u>aptize, <u>bl</u>ossoms/<u>bl</u>anket):

wind chimes and church bells
cleanse the air; in the gutter
blossoms mixed with grit

wind chimes and church bells
baptize us; in the gutter
blossoms blanket grit

A **simile** compares two things using "like" or "as."

your smile sweet as cotton candy

You can use similes to enhance your writing. Fill in the blanks for the following words and then try adding a simile to your next poem. Once you get used to seeing similarities between things, it won't be too hard to develop metaphors for your writing as well.

Sharp as... _____

_____

_____

Quiet as... _____

_____

_____

Hot like... _____

_____

_____

Tall as... _____

_____

_____

Soft as... _____

_____

_____

Sweet as... _____

_____

_____

Shiny as... _____

_____

_____

Delicate as...

_____

_____

_____

Strong like...

_____

_____

_____

Fast as...

_____

_____

_____

Smooth as...

_____

_____

_____

Bitter as...

_____

_____

_____

Make a List

Sometimes writing a poem is as easy as making a list. Write down the first three words that come to mind when you think of home. You can pull words from the cloud you made earlier. My list looks like this:

> home is
> complicated
> familiar
> & bittersweet

Home is   _____

              _____

              _____

Now try using two words instead of one.

> home is
> complicated comfort
> familiar faces
> bittersweet memories

Home is   _____   _____

              _____   _____

              _____   _____

Now compose a short phrase using five words or less.

> home is an elusive dream

Home is   _____

            _____

            _____

I used my short phrase as the foundation of my poem. Home represents comfort and safety for many people but for African Americans and other groups, home is complicated. I wanted my poem to reflect that reality.

> home is an elusive dream
> for those born without
> sanctuary

Write a short poem about what home means to you:

_____

_____

_____

_____

_____

_____

_____

Savor Each Season

My favorite season is autumn but I find inspiration in nature all year round. I love to write haiku because they're short and the rules are easy to remember: 5-7-5. With this Japanese poem, you can take a quick snapshot of a scene in nature—or you can write about any topic in an economical way. You just need to count out your syllables: five on the first line, seven on the second line, and five more on the final line of your poem.

When I'm writing haiku, I put my hand on the desk (palm down). Then I use my fingertips to tap out the syllables for each word. You can also clap or tap your toe—whatever helps you count 5-7-5.

joy = one syllable

happy = two syllables

happiness = three syllables

tulips bring me joy (5 syllables)

lifting their heads to the sun (7 syllables)

drinking in the light (5 syllables)

solace is the sound

of a robin's bright song on

a bleak winter day

thickly falling snow

drapes me in delicate lace

snowflakes veil my eyes

winter sun teases,

sprouting hope in a body

weary of the cold

serenity spreads

like a smooth white blanket of

freshly fallen snow

birds chatter at dawn

summoning a new season

with incantations

I wake to the sound

of a dove's melancholy

salute to the sun

Try writing your own haiku. You can pull words from the clouds you created on the previous pages.

_____ (5)

_____ (7)

_____ (5)

_____ (5)

_____ (7)

_____ (5)

_____ (5)

_____ (7)

_____ (5)

_____ (5)

_____ (7)

_____ (5)

20

_____ (5)

_____ (7)

_____ (5)

_____ (5)

_____ (7)

_____ (5)

_____ (5)

_____ (7)

_____ (5)

_____ (5)

_____ (7)

_____ (5)

_____ (5)

_____ (7)

_____ (5)

_____ (5)

_____ (7)

_____ (5)

_____ (5)

_____ (7)

_____ (5)

_____ (5)

_____ (7)

_____ (5)

Free Verse

I love to write free verse poetry because there are NO rules! It's fun to try writing different kinds of poems—like a haiku or a sonnet. But sometimes I want my ideas to flow freely and that's when I write free verse poetry. No rhyme scheme? No problem! No punctuation? That's okay! Many of my free verse poems don't have titles. No title? No problem!

I wrote this poem after logging off Facebook because my feed was full of bad news.

> sometimes I want to
> lay down my sword & shield
> but where is the refuge
> for a weary soldier
> who is tired of fighting
> but not ready
> to die

I don't have a car, which means I do a lot of walking in the city. Most of the time I'm lost in my own thoughts and my feet are on autopilot. I have to remind myself to look around and be present, which is why I wrote this poem.

> if you do not pause
> the forsythia will leaf
> and the cherry tree's blossoms
> will drift into the gutter
> and swirl down the sewer
> before you even realize
> that spring is here

On my way to the bank last spring I stopped to admire a young apple tree. I pulled my phone out and took a few pictures but couldn't capture the tree's beauty, so I went home and wrote this poem.

the sapling

its canopy of blossoms
sifts sunlight like lace
if only we each could have
one moment
once a year
to bloom just as humbly
blushing in our own
perfection

Easter is a holiday that people often associate with chocolate bunnies, pastel-colored eggs, and marshmallow chicks. As a child, Easter meant a new dress for church, fragrant white lilies on the altar, and dinner afterward with my grandparents. I spend most holidays on my own now and wrote this poem after waking up to news of the terrorist attacks in Colombo.

easter

this morning
I am bleeding
and there is a river
of blood flowing
in sri lanka
christ isn't the only one
waking up with wounds

Sometimes I give myself advice...

know your worth
and take no less
than you deserve—
no discounts
no freebees
no layaway

And sometimes I try to offer encouragement to others...

even if you can't
hear my voice
know that I am
rooting for you
praising your name
lifting you up in prayer
and waiting for you
on the other side
of the finish line

This concrete or visual poem started out as a prose poem; I wrote it as a paragraph but wasn't satisfied, so I tried a format that mimics the steps of an escalator. I used to run track and this exchange with a woman I didn't know reminded me of passing the baton to a teammate in a relay race.

Relay

                                       her phone
                                     dropped
                                 ahead of me
                           the sister
                      the train
                   trying to catch
              the escalator
         running up
                                                 for the train
                                            & kept heading
                                       without a word
                                 back around
                           then she turned
                      to pick it up
                 saw me stooping
            stopped & turned
       she cursed
                                                 onto the train
                                          would make it
                                     holding her phone
                                that my hand
                         to make sure
                    she held the door
               the same way
          was going
     knowing I

Try writing your own free verse poems. Remember—there are no rules!

_____

_____

_____

_____

_____

_____

_____

_____

_____

_____

_____

Star Power

I wrote this poem after one of my favorite artists passed away. Whenever I need a confidence boost, I head over to YouTube and watch Prince's jaw-dropping guitar solo at the 2004 Hall of Fame Induction Ceremony. The poem begins with words from a character in Alice Walker's 1982 novel *The Color Purple*.

Shug said...

I think
it pisses God off
if you don't notice
the color purple
so I always stop for crocuses
lilacs and grape hyacinth
but then I find myself
missing Prince
and wish he were still
standing just offstage
in his black pinstripe suit
and red fedora
ready to humble
them with his brilliance
leave us gaping in awe
and shining with pride
before offering his guitar
up to the gods and
strutting offstage
collar up

Think of your favorite artist. How do you feel when you listen to their music? Did you see Beyoncé's 2018 Coachella performance? Whether you're a fan or not, create a word cloud below:

Beyonce'

Last year I wrote my shortest poem ever:

even Beyoncé

Analyze this poem. What do you think it means? Should it have a title?

_____

_____

_____

_____

_____

_____

_____

_____

_____

Now try writing your own free verse poem about your favorite artist. Think about the sound of their voice, how they look onstage, how they move, and how their music makes you feel.

_____

_____

_____

_____

_____

_____

_____

_____

_____

_____

Create a portrait of your favorite artist. You can draw a picture of them, or create a collage using magazine images and words. Add some glitter! For inspiration, go online and check out the stunning portraits created by Mickalene Thomas and Makeeba "Keebs" Rainey.

Write a Letter

One way to write a poem is to start by writing something else—like a letter. Think about someone who made an impact on your life. If you wrote that person a letter, what would you say? Is there a skill they taught you that you still use today? Did you share an experience that still brings a smile to your face? How would you thank them?

Dear _____,

_____

_____

_____

_____

_____

_____

_____

_____

Extract the Essence

Now that you've written your letter, read it over and circle ten words that represent the <u>essence</u> of your message. What are the most important words you used? Which words capture the emotion you expressed in your letter?

1. _____

2. _____

3. _____

4. _____

5. _____

6. _____

7. _____

8. _____

9. _____

10. _____

Now use these essential words to compose a poem:

_____

_____

_____

_____

_____

_____

_____

_____

_____

_____

_____

_____

Honor an Ancestor

Write a letter to an ancestor—a relative who has passed on or someone who sacrificed in the past to make sure things would be better for future generations. How would you thank them? What would you want them to know about the world you live in today?

Dear _____,

_____

_____

_____

_____

_____

_____

_____

_____

_____

Now that you've written your letter, read it over and circle ten words that represent the <u>essence</u> of your message. What are the most important words you used? Which words capture the emotion you expressed in your letter?

1. _____

2. _____

3. _____

4. _____

5. _____

6. _____

7. _____

8. _____

9. _____

10. _____

Now use these essential words to compose a poem:

_____

_____

_____

_____

_____

_____

_____

_____

_____

_____

_____

_____

I wrote this elegy for Sandra Bland, an African American activist who died in police custody in 2015. The phoenix is one of my favorite mythical creatures because as the bird dies in flames, a new phoenix is born from the ashes. I was also inspired by something I once heard feminist icon Gloria Steinem say in a television interview: she didn't believe in passing the torch to a younger leader—it made more sense to share your light with as many people as possible.

The first version of this poem had plenty of adjectives but I decided to strip them away. I'm not entirely satisfied with this version and will probably revise it again.

The Phoenix Lives

you held your torch high
to guide us through the shadows
but they too saw your shine
and could not let your beacon stand

they tried to douse your fire
but your love for us only burned brighter
from your pyre sprang sparks
that lit a thousand torches
and those will burn
forever

Honor Wreath

Place a photograph of someone you admire in the center of the page. It could be a relative, an ancestor, or a leader (past or present) that you respect. Circle the photo with words, symbols, and objects that pay tribute to your role model.

Take a Stand

How do you feel about immigration? The climate crisis? Gun violence? The people running your country? As an immigrant I have written several poems about the US president's determination to build a wall along the border with Mexico. Some people think poetry should only be about the beauty of nature, but poets write about all the things that matter to them. Think about an issue that matters to you. Write about what's causing the problem and how you think it can be solved.

_____

_____

_____

_____

_____

_____

_____

_____

_____

_____

_____

_____

_____

_____

_____

Now that you've written your statement, read it over and circle ten words that represent the <u>essence</u> of your point of view. What are the most important words you used?

1. _____

2. _____

3. _____

4. _____

5. _____

6. _____

7. _____

8. _____

9. _____

10. _____

Now use these essential words to compose a poem:

_____

_____

_____

_____

_____

_____

_____

_____

_____

_____

_____

_____

Ten-Day Poetry Challenge

You've learned how to find inspiration, how to get warmed up, and how to turn prose into poetry. Now you're ready to make poetry a daily practice!

There are lots of different types of poems. Some have a lot of rules and some don't—explore and choose the one that's right for you. Don't be afraid to try something new! Your poems don't have to be perfect. This is an opportunity to find new ways to express yourself.

acrostic
sonnet
ekphrasis
haiku
free verse
concrete poetry
elegy
tanka
limerick
ode

The Poetry Foundation has an excellent website where you can find a glossary of poetic terms and thousands of poems to inspire you: www.poetryfoundation.org.

If you need some encouragement, read poet JP Howard's excellent advice: https://link.medium.com/1vUqQol4hW.

Most importantly, have fun! Share your poems with friends and family. And keep going—once you've filled up the pages of this book, get a notebook and keep on writing. You don't have to wait for April to try writing thirty poems in thirty days...

Day 1

_____

_____

_____

_____

_____

_____

_____

_____

_____

_____

_____

Day 2

Day 3

Day 4

Day 5

Day 6

Day 7

Day 8

Day 9

Day 10

Doodle!

About the Author

Zetta Elliott moved to the US in 1994 to pursue her PhD in American Studies at NYU. She is the author of over thirty books for young readers. Her poetry has been published in several anthologies, including *We Rise, We Resist, We Raise Our Voices* and *New Daughters of Africa*; her own young adult poetry collection, *Say Her Name*, will be published by Jump at the Sun in 2020. Elliott is an advocate for greater diversity and equity in children's literature; her essays on race and publishing have appeared in *The Huffington Post*, *School Library Journal*, and *Publishers Weekly*. She currently lives in Philadelphia.

Learn more at
www.zettaelliott.com

Made in the USA
Middletown, DE
16 September 2021